Down the l

D0708228

CELIA BERRIDGE

Kingfisher Books

Advisers: Betty Grubb (Nursery Headteacher),
Patricia Brown (Children's Librarian)

First published in 1987 by Kingfisher Books Ltd
Elsley Court, 20–22 Great Titchfield Street
London W1P 7AD
A Grisewood and Dempsey Company

BRITISH LIBRARY CATALOGUING IN PUBLICATION DATA
Down the road—(Stepping stones)
    1. Human ecology—Great Britain—Juvenile literature
    I. Berridge, Celia   II. Series
    333.7 ′ 0941   GF551
ISBN: 0 86272 245 4

Edited by Vanessa Clarke
Cover designed by Pinpoint Design Company
Phototypeset by Tradespools Ltd,
Frome, Somerset
Printed in Spain

Mum and I are going down the road
to my friend's house.

The lift door opens. Swish!

We can go faster if I sit in my buggy.

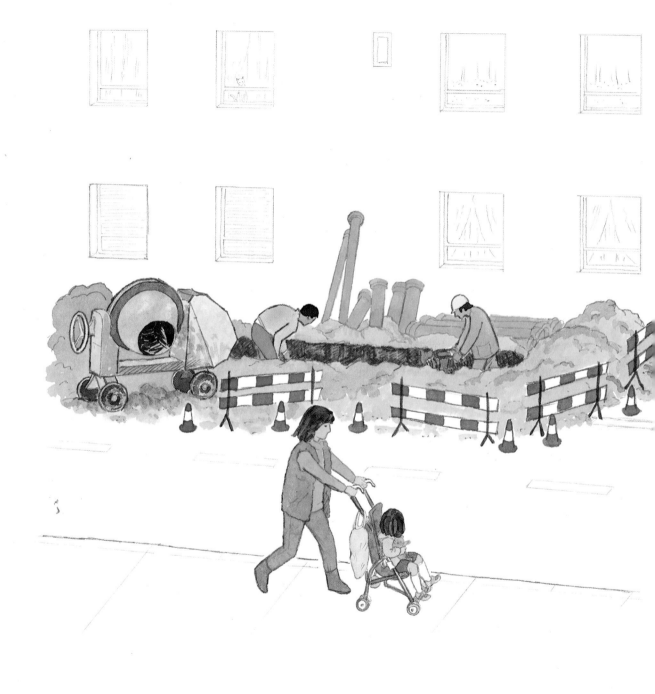

Off we go down the road. Look, Mum!
I can see a great big hole.

What a noise! That man is digging up the
road with the drill.

And that big shovel is scooping up all the
earth and stones.

Crash. Bang! The dustmen are throwing
rubbish into the dustcart.

Look at that big red fire engine. I can hear
its loud siren.

Here are the traffic lights. We wait here for the lights to change.

Look! The cars have stopped and the green light says we can cross safely.

Now we are walking past the shops. But
we are not going shopping today.

Look who I can see, Mum? It's my friend
and her Mum with their dog.

This is the greengrocer's shop. I hold onto
my buggy while Mum buys some flowers.

My friend lives down this road.
Who's that calling "Hello"?
Mum, it's your friend waving to us.

I can see pretty pink blossom in the tree.
Look, Mum!

We stop and see if anything's coming
before we cross the road again.

Here we are at my friend's house. I'm going
inside to play. Goodbye!